ON THE VERGE

By Peres Owino

To mom and dad,
from your offspring

Politics

**Hey! HEY! We don't do Politically Correct here.
You can take that crap somewhere else.**

Guess what? You <u>DO</u> have the power

No More Phuckery

Earth and its inhabitants have been the topic of discussion at the Annual Intra Galactic Alliance Assembly meetings for the past two thousand years. There has been a general concern among the members of the Alliance that the human race is unleashing a tremendous amount of phuckery upon the Earth.

It is the opinion of all members of the Alliance, excluding Earthlings whose IQ levels are below Assembly standards, that these lower beings are not consuming bovines fast enough. The Neptunians and Uranians are extremely peeved by the amount of methane gas being unleashed by the Earth dwelling bovines, as the gaseous matter fogs up their planets every 150 days when Jupiter and Saturn step out of the way putting them in Earth's general direction.

After extensive debate, the IGA passed the Phuckery Eradication Act by a two vote margin. This Act required the Martians, the only members with kick ass gadgets capable of annihilating the entire galaxy and the Plutocrats, believers in diplomacy, to land on planet Earth and swiftly eradicate its gaseous problem. If the Plutocrats' diplomatic tactics proved insufficient, the Martians were authorized to take over and wipe out the human race with their biological chemicals.

But the Jupitean Conglomerate threw their cloak into the debate. Fornicators and purveyors of all things perverse, the Jupitean emissary stated "the time for diplomacy has long passed; there is no need for the Plutocrats in this battle. Reason must make way for much torture and physical dismemberment. That is good learning for underlings." He received a great deal of hoorahs from his own kind. The Mercurians, known far seers, looked into the future and saw the true intent of the Jupiteans and it was decided that their debauchery must not be exported beyond the borders of Pasiphae and Sinope, Jupiter's outermost moons.

After a six hundred year stalemate, a coin toss decided who would accompany the Martians, whose place on the ship, no one dared debate. The Saturnians, Spiritually Superior snobs, wanted no part of this "kick the Earthlings ass campaign!" So it came as no surprise that they won the coin toss.

A few days later the IGA's convoy pointed their meteor-like spacecraft towards their preferred landing pad on Earth, the pyramids at Manchu Pinchu, Peru. But the whole operation hit a snag when, due to the Martians miscalculation of the earth's shift since their last visit, the convoy found itself descending upon a primitive tribe in Iowa's southern region, unleashing their entire cargo of biological chemicals. Needless to say, the disgruntled Saturnians were thoroughly unamused. Apparently, the Martians refused to ask for directions.

Footage from Earth shows much vomiting and diarrhea. The plan was half successful, all things considered.

Crap or get off the pot!!!

Political activity is the right, no, the responsibility of EVERY citizen. I care not whether the future looks so bright you've got to wear shades or it's as dark as the womb you lay dormant in for 9 months. YOU must take part in the ebb and flow of your nation. Otherwise, when shit hits the fan, refrain from complaining as you were never part of the solution from the start.

Town Hall

I have just returned from a Town Hall Meeting in Sherman Oaks, CA. Well, if I am to be 100% honest let me call it what it was, a Town Hall Brawl. Most of the people in the room were north of 40 years old, white and male; but I figured I could take them. Hey, I have no problem drop kicking grandpa in self-defense.

Nose tipped and glad to be a Negro rep, I made my way towards the Performing Arts Center of some high school whose name I don't care to remember. It was not until I reached the steps that I realized I was heading in the direction of some shit. To step into or not to step into? Tough choice. I decided to step and low and behold a skinny gentleman—who looked more like an amalgamation of any of the four major races—handed me a magazine with the face of Barack Obama adorned with a Hitler moustache. Yes, Papi had that much cajones! THEY figured a "minority" handing out controversial pamphlets about a "minority" president to other "minorities" is less likely to encounter a fist in face or foot in ass response because we are both "minorities." THEY were right. Don't you just hate it when THEY are right?

See the way I saw it, I had a bigger battle to fight so slugging it out with the local idiot would have only affected MY credibility. I took the pamphlet, smiled and went inside. The room was packed! I mean it was so packed people were sitting in the aisles and on the stage behind the Congressman. Once the floor was opened for questions, the Old Western unruly cowboy mentality that pissed off every Clint Eastwood character from "A Fistful of Dollars" to "Unforgiven" reared its ugly head. The only differences were these guys were neither in a saloon nor inebriated.

With the shoe-size attitude came shoe-size questions and reasoning. Logic was officially replaced with emotion, and folks were throwing out the baby with the bath water. "Personal liberty," a fundamental right that Americans

10

clutch on to like bad teeth to braces was violated once every ten seconds. Anyone who asked a question that someone in the hall opposed was booed. Some folks were booed just for something to do. There were times when six people were talking at the same time; one was confused as to whether they were assisting the Congressman answer the question asked or just suffering from a severe case of verbal tourettes.

Then came the true weakest link, the possible missing link between man and ape. This young man asked the one question that seems to have more lives than a cat: the President's citizenship. Immigration 101 – If you are born in the United States or BORN TO A U.S. CITIZEN who meets certain requirements, YOU ARE BORN A U.S. CITIZEN! This information is not hard to find, just go here like I did: http://travel.state.gov/law/info/info_609.html. Next question, PLEASE! And not a moment too soon.

An angrier, older male made his way to the microphone and began reading a speech attacking Barack Obama's Healthcare Bill. HALT!!! If you missed it, stop reading right now and follow the link below to a video you need: http://www.youtube.com/watch?v=mEJL2Uuv-oQ.

Let me summarize. When an issue such as Healthcare reaches critical mass (i.e. enough people are pissed off), a member of Congress or the President can decide to take on that issue and make legal changes. First, a committee is formed in Capitol Hill (Legislative Branch) to tackle the issue and they generate a bill. Once in agreement, it moves to the House of Representatives. If passed, it moves to the Senate. If passed, it gets to the President's desk (Executive Branch). If he doesn't like it, the bill gets a veto and the process begins all over again. If he likes it, it becomes law and the responsibility of the Executive Branch to enforce the law. Once a bill becomes law it is the job of courts (Judicial Branch) to make sure it is upheld. See how that works? The President does not generate bills; he can only sign them into law. If you hate the direction a bill is heading, guess who needs to be fired? Exactly. Your Congress-man or woman.

People, the answers are out there and easily accessible. There is no sense, literally, in getting emotionally wrapped up in the wrong information. You have to learn how the system works in order to fix the broken parts. Otherwise you might just pull out the bolt that is holding this phucker together. Then what do you have? Stop choking on your own ignorance. It is an ugly way to die.

Silence

Apathy and complacency are enmity to democracy. A system based on the people, for the people, by the people inevitably meets its demise when the people remain silent in fear, real or imagined. There is silence between the lines in the newspapers, silence amidst the political pauses, silence in the channel surfing. There is silence when nothing is questioned.

Politically Correct

I'm exhausted and yet I wonder about this 100-pound gorilla in the room. Does anyone notice it or is the general consensus to ignore it? Politically correct—now there is an oxymoron if I ever heard one. Whose grand idea was it to institute it in the first place? And how can anything political be correct? Politics has nothing to do with right or wrong but the popular and the unpopular.

And is it a violation of the freedom of speech if you are forced to suppress your speech? I mean, are another man's words that threatening to you? What the heck happened to the spine of this nation? When did emotion take over reason? I thought that democracy was of the people. If the people are unable to express themselves openly, what do we have? Certainly not democracy, or anything close to it.

This applies specifically to "White" (whatever that means) America. What happened? How did you get to the point where everyone else can say anything they want about you but you are not allowed to defend yourself or even think of uttering sentiments in the same vein? Has the playing field been leveled or merely set in favor of others? How is it that 61.7% of the population feels backed up against a wall when it comes to speaking their mind?

Yeah, yeah, "slavery and the proceeding racism," we all know the lyrics to that song.

But when will we work towards solutions that fix the problem not create new ones? How does stripping someone else of their power help balance things out? Logic states that we are creating a fertile ground for bitterness and anger and it is only a matter of time before the oppressed rise up and kick you squarely in the nuts or tits depending on how high the kick goes!

We need not worry about the potential threat we are creating abroad; there is sufficient cause for concern within.

The Grass is Greener

What is this need we have to have an opinion about other people? Why do you care about Tom Cruise's daughter or the Jolie-Pitt kids? Do you want to raise them? I don't.

Yet I have to admit that the infidelity scandals are pretty saucy. From the Congress of the House to the Woody Tiger to California's Sperminator, the sordid details of marital deceit get juicier by the minute. Can Hollywood afford all those movie rights?

And God forgive the "Good Wives" for standing beside their men in a show of support. I will take this moment to thank Ms. Governator and Ms. Sanford for standing for something greater than a cheating spouse's dignity, THEIR OWN dignity.

Could this one nation under God, built on family values, which include monogamy and 1 Corinthians 3:15 type love, be crushing under God's weight?

Mirky Waters

Mirky BLACKWATER *is the most comprehensive, professional, military, law enforcement, security, peacekeeping, and stability operations company in the world.* **Mirky BLACKWATER** *comprises nine separate business units to offer the most comprehensive professional security, peacekeeping, and stability operations company in the world*

VISION

To SUPPORT security, PEACE, freedom, and DEMOCRACY everywhere.

I have often found it strange that soldiers would be perceived as agents of peace and democracy. 'Security' I can understand but support, by definition, means to assist something already in existence, making the presence of this trained mercenary in Iraq or any other country for that matter a beast of great suspicion. But if you think their vision raises some eyebrows, take a look at their mission statement.

MISSION

To support national and **INTERNATIONAL SECURITY POLICIES** *that protect those who are* **DEFENSELESS** *and provide a free voice for all with a dedication to providing* **ETHICAL,** *efficient, and effective turnkey solutions that positively impact the lives of those still caught in desperate times.*

How do you support security policies in a nation fraught with suicide bombings, political instability, sectarian violence and armed rebellions by freedom fighters? The answer to that question is: one can't support something not

16

in existence.

Now, go with me on this. Here's a chance to make your brain hurt.

Since security does not exist in Iraq and one can only offer support to what is in existence, does it mean that these mercenaries are supporting anarchy? They have been implicated in several acts of violence in Iraq. I wonder; do they adhere to any international security policies? Are they accountable to any government, international body or higher power? Are multi-national co-operations becoming more important than borders and sovereignty?

Mirky BLACKWATER *is committed to the foot soldiers -- the men and women who stand on the frontlines of the global war on terror and who believe in a peaceful future for their communities and nations.*

Didn't you say earlier that your mission was to "protect those who are defenseless?" That would be the unarmed civilians not the armed guards.

And may I just add that Iraq was not part of the terror belt until a certain swaggering Texan became president and decided to "bring 'em on!" Yeah, he was trying to relive the glory days of gun-toting Puritans shooting their way across the great plains, killing off Indians armed only with tomahawks and their word.

Whether serving in or out of uniform, **Mirky BLACKWATER** *is committed to providing these men and women with the very best in training and tactical support to ensure they are fully prepared to meet current and future global security challenges.*

Hmm... in or out of uniform. Out of uniform... seems to be the insurgent dress code of choice. Well, birds of a feather...

Amendment

All candidates seeking to serve in the US Senate and House of Representatives are required to have at least one immediate family member enlisted in the US Military to qualify for a seat.

This is a check and balance initiative aimed at preventing preemptive strikes on sovereign nations by ensuring due process of the law and thinking twice before blowing Junior to bits.

***

Any organization or random gathering of humans requiring its own acronym and flag is really a sovereign entity in and of itself and cannot be trusted to work for the good of anyone NOT affiliated with their flag.

***

Patriot Act

FEAR

Which of these will you stand up against?

Love Letter To America

Dear America,

Someone once asked me for a foreign perspective to this question, 'Has desegregation failed?'

If we find that one community is held back in its pursuit of proper educational, social and political growth, due to segregation then desegregation must be viewed as an option, right? Well, desegregation was implemented but the problems persist, meaning something else is at play. Therefore, attempting to answer this question with a simple "yes" or "no" is to overlook the inherent nature of man.

Man, in the general sense, prefers to associate himself with members of the same species, others being less intelligent or more aggressive than him. Putting this under a microscope, we find that man is also most comfortable among members of his family. Of course this does not apply to dysfunctional families, hence the prefix 'dys.'

The former being the case, man further subdivides himself into peer groups, these being made up of persons who share the same interests, traditions and goals. Over time and due to the changing priorities of society, traditions and goals are judged materialistically. Henceforth, persons of the same financial bracket have become members of the same social bracket.

These social brackets congregate to create their individual living quarters. Now, due to the unequal allocation of resources, we find that the majority of the wealth is in the hand of the Caucasian populous. They have used this wealth to put up living quarters that they believe best exemplify their financial status. What this has done is not only created but perpetuated a status quo in society. The pivotal question is this, 'was this intentional'? You decide.

The underlying quandary with our communities is therefore not segregation but the unequal distribution of resources. Believe me, if all races were well equipped with elements of a better living, if you could not tell the difference between Bel-Air and Compton, segregation would be a non-issue.

It is imperative that we lay the blame where it lies. Social institutions have been desegregated, but they are still in perpetual decline. Why? Not because there are not enough white kids or African Americans to depict the demographic of American society, but because they are under funded. We must put aside this sing song about race and deal with the true issue: America is currently experiencing the greatest division between the haves and the wants and race is merely a deliberate camouflage.

A Politician
One who surveys a conflict between two opposing sides and manipulates the situation to create a resolution that best suits the needs and desires of his constituency a.k.a. the folks that paid for my ticket.

A Diplomat
One who surveys a conflict between two opposing sides and manipulates the situation to create a solution that best suits the needs and the desires of both parties.

An Idealist
One who surveys a conflict between two opposing sides and manipulates the situation to create a solution that suits what he believes to be the needs and desires of a perfect society.

An Idiot
One who surveys a conflict between two opposing sides and does nothing.

Election Candidates:
All Reproductive Organs Mutually Represented

Now, let's figure this one out together.

It is election season and all reproductive organs are mutually represented. Most of them are howling at the moon chanting, "government is incompetent, big and bloated" while running for a government position.

If that is the case, why shouldn't the voting public assume you, the candidate, are incompetent, big and bloated? After all, you are running for a slot in government and if incompetent, big and bloated is the norm then it must inevitably be the prerequisite, no?

Why else would someone spend millions of dollars to be part of an institution or organization they have little or no respect for unless they were incompetent?

Wouldn't RESIGNING the very moment said candidate was declared the winner be a better way to get the point across? They would actually be reducing the size of government AND our taxes coz that's one less person we have to pay?

Unless of course they are lying, insane, lying, unethical or yes, LYING.

If you are going to deceive your way into public office, at least take the time to assume that some portion of the voting public is intelligent enough to sniff you out! That goes double for the stiletto coalition. And here we thought Palin was the only uterus we had to worry about. The Witch, The Gums, The Tomboy and the Wrestler are all Palinettes. Clearly the Hillary movement birthed no one.

The True America

The True America is beyond the geographical boundaries to its east, west, north and south. It exists well beyond the coasts of the Pacific and the Atlantic. For America, the ideology is universal, representing equality, justice, life, liberty and the pursuit of happiness. Ideals held dear by all men and thought to be self-evident long before there was a notion of America.

Therefore, no man is entitled to America. True America is entitled to ALL MEN!

***

Know your history!

If a wealthy landowner organized his field hands into a revolutionary army and paid them to help him fight off a colonial ruler threatening his land, for whose benefit is the war being waged?

If that same wealthy landowner, after expelling the colonialists, then sets up a government to ensure that his authority is never challenged again, who is that wealthy land owner's remaining threat?

If the same wealthy landowner's land, wealth and system of government is passed on to his children for forty-four generations without change, who is shocked that we are where we are today?

People, don't be fooled. A fruit always rots from within.

Critical Mass

What is Critical Mass? If you have heard the word before but do not understand its meaning I applaud you for being aware. I hope you will take the time to investigate its meaning and apply it to your life.

For those who have never heard of it, I will assume you are without an ounce of political interest and it is to you that all fingers must point when it comes to blaming someone for the downward spiral of all things civic, a direct consequence of political ambivalence.

Critical Mass: the existence of sufficient momentum in a social system that becomes self-sustaining, fueling further growth. The impetus for change is not merely the awareness of one or even millions, but the awareness and the thrust of more than one but less than a million. It took the ramblings of one person and less than a million petitions to evoke and sustain the eradication of prayer in schools. That small number was all the critical mass the issue needed in a nation of 300 million.

Jesus only needed 12 to revolutionize and sustain how the world would come to view man's relationship to God. Twelve was the critical mass that shifted some from Judaism to Christianity. That and a sword.

Let's take this moment to review all that has been going on in the Middle East in the past months. That, my friend, is the power of critical mass. That is how you do democracy. Isn't it ironic how the same "Arabs" who "hate us for our freedom," (a statement uttered by a President whose election should have drawn some critical mass) are showing us just how to exercise freedom?

In the past five years, the US has exhibited exemplary critical mass in several issues:

The non-partisan Tea Party ushered in a new era of "pissed off politics" electing mostly Republicans into office. Great work! Except now the same Republicans are reneging on the Tea Party Caucus evite. Who didn't see that coming?

Then there was the scandalous revealings of the Woody Tiger. And oh how the slighted mistresses came out in mass asking for apologies from the very publicly married Tiger, while the truly slighted spouse went into hiding! Every woman with a uterus had an opinion. Critical mass led the Tiger to make a public apology to us for cheating on his wife. We didn't need it, but we made him feel like we did.

My favourite was the push to get the Lindsey hanged. There were cries from celeb-haters and everyone who ever lost someone to drunk driving to get her behind bars. Thanks to critical mass, she briefly spent some time in the big house. Briefly.

And one from the archives: Don Immus and his "nappy headed whores." Word on the street was we needed to be offended by this, especially if you were a woman of a darker hue. Thanks to critical mass, he briefly lost his job. Briefly. I bet you these girls' playlists include songs with "whore" reference. But I guess Don is a "white guy" and for them, standards are different.

But the greatest show of critical mass in the US came courtesy of Michael Vick and his dawgs. Paris could have killed a human being while driving under the influence, but Michael Vick's crime was a warning of a "pending psychotic snap." His thirst for blood was "clearly" being manifested in his feverish funding of illegal dog-fights.

These sorts of media analysis of Mr. Vick helped traumatized animal lovers envision a young strapping buck sporting a chinchilla coat and gator shoes, peering over his five hundred dollar leather-rimmed sun-glasses at the whimpering pit bulls trained to go for the jugular.

He rubs his hands maniacally, an illegal Cuban cigar dangling seductively off his "Ham cursed" full lips, succulent from the chicken he had for dinner an hour ago. He wipes a spec of dust from his pimp style white suit, nods his head and the games begin. The dogs leap at each other's throats! Tonight, one of them will die.

But I wonder. Where was the critical mass for the 2000 elections or the preemptive strike on Iraq and the bullshit that came with it? Or when Julian Assange's freedom was threatened for doing what the media is supposed to do? Where is critical mass with regards to Private First Class Bradley Manning?

Let's add insult to injury here. Lindsay's poor judgment led to incarceration while Scott Libby's act of treason led to a presidential pardon. Where is the pissed off public when justice is really being tramped?

Who really cares about the private life of toe-tapping-anti-same-sex-marriage-except-in-public-bathrooms -picking-up-a-piece-of-toilet-paper Idaho Senator Larry Craig? Are we here to monitor the hypocrites or uphold justice? Well, that one is tricky.

Then here comes the NAACP with a funeral for the "N" word, a token of critical mass. "We are gathered here today to bid farewell to a much despised word." Huh? Do we not see that it is the pomp and circumstance that gives a thing power? Why hold a ceremony for a word you despise instead of simply ignoring it? Is it really about change or is it about "drama"?

The gospel according to Rumsfeld takes us beyond the "known unknowns" to the "unknown unknowns". Yes, there are things out there you don't know you don't know. And we must be at peace with this blissful ignorance, accepting life as it is, questioning nothing and going to war with the army we have, not the army we might like." No critical mass present.

I could go on for pages and only touch upon the crazies of the past 5 years. The Wall Street bailout and AIG Bonuses – talk about money defying physics and trickling up. George Tenet's legacy that resulted in a Medal of Freedom, millions of Allied Forces, Afghans and Iraqis lives and book sales. Mark Foley's love for young pages and his insult to alcoholics the world over. Randy "Duke"

Cunningham, Abu Gareb's, Tom Delay, Club Gitmo (now there is a way to damn down torture), Haliburton, Haditha massacre, Gas prices, Jack Abramoff, GI Suicides, Bob Ney, Blackwater aka Xe, The Gulf States post Katrina, Global warming, Teachers wages, Homeless veterans, Dafur, Sex trafficking, Alberto Gonzales' memory lapses and Senator McCain's "gay" sweaters. Where was the critical mass? Wait, these topics are too political, and if there is one thing Americans don't do, it's politics.

So let's go back to what really matters: Bishop Eddie Long's tight shirts, The Trump's long form birth certificate, the Sperminator's maid in America, and the girl who showed off her naked booty at the Key club a week ago.

Ignorance

Ignorance is not bliss but a cancer that metastasizes throughout society and fosters racism, sexism, the reality TV craze, Paris Hilton's career, pre-emptive wars, genocide, corruption and all the bad portions of human history.

***

There is a difference between ignorance and stupidity.
Ignorance is the absence of knowledge.
Stupidity is the absence of acknowledgement.
For the latter there is no hope.

Ignorance is Hereditary

I think the problem with the public education system stems from the old national policy of Isolationism. We managed to instill that policy so perfectly on the individual level that the average American does not know his neighbour, what state borders his own, or the name of any sitting judge on the Supreme Court. And these are the adults.

They, however, are familiar with Oprah, Simon and Lady Gaga. Why? Coz these folks exist within the individually isolated boundaries. The connections may be superficial at best but they are there, influencing and making an impact. And these are the adults. Maybe we should consider electing our Presidents on *America's Got Talent*.

Folks, we can't blame the kids for being disconnected because the apple never falls far from the tree.

Terrorists

Terror: Extreme *fear*
Deepest fear - *Loss*
Loss -   Of life and *sustenance*
Sustenance -   Food, clothing, shelter

Terrorism: Use of violence and *intimidation*
Intimidation - *Influence* by frightening
Influence -   *Effect* a person or thing has
               on another
Effect -   *Impression*
Impression -   Suspicion produced in the
               mind

Terrorize: *Coerce* by terrorism
Coerce -   *Compel* by threat or force
Compel -   *Pressure*
Pressure -   Oppressive influence

Terrorist: Creates the *suspicion* of extreme *fear*
through the use of *force* or threats
   Intimidates into an impression of the *loss
   of sustenance* through *coercion*

So TERROR, in its broadest sense is an externally applied pressure that leaves an impression that one's sustenance is threatened.

Terrorists can therefore be:
   UN Security Council if you are North Korea
   Western Imperialist if you are from the East
   Gaddaffi's Regime if you are a Libyan Rebel
   Islamic Radicals if you are Christian Radical
   Christian Radicals if you are Islamic Radical
   Pro-Life fanatics if you are a Pro-Choice Fanatic
   Pro-War fanatics if you are Anti-War

Anti-War supporters if you are Pro-War
America if you are from a CIA backed coup country
NAFTA if you are a worker
FBI if you are militia
Gays if you are Anti-Gay marriage
Black if you are White Supremacist
Bullies if you are a Nerd

This list is endless.

SCORE CARD

Religious Death Tolls
He who is without sin, let him cast the first stone.

In The Name of God

Spanish Inquisition	23,000,000
Middle Ages	15,000,000
The Pilgrims Progress	5,000
Crusades	150,000,000
Conquering the Americas	114,000,000
Colonization of Africa	48,000,000
TOTAL	**348,105,000**

In The Name Of Allah

Crusades	32,000
Ottoman Empire	?
Armenian Genocide	1,500,000
Terrorism	?
Terrorism since 9/11	16,789
Slave Trade	11,000,000
Dafur	1,900,000
TOTAL	**~15,160,000**

Don't blame the Islamic fundamentalists. They are just trying to catch up.

Sex

This section is neither a sex toy,
nor a substitute for one.
Please read it with all your clothes on.
Thank you.

Sleeping, eating and fucking are our three main functions. Of course, the Catholic Church's sole objective is to prove to the world that we can do with a limit on these by modulating the first, regulating the second and eradicating the third. But we know better. See, back in the day, survival depended on these three activities and that dependency is forever stamped onto our DNA. (Not to mention, all three provide some level of satisfaction). With all these in check, all we had to worry about were the dinosaurs. (yep! This is not my idea of a segue either, but we must be content).

The Post-Coital Backslide Into Friendship

Is it possible to ENJOY a passionate swapping of body fluids with another human being then swiftly regress back into the dark abyss of "just friends"?

If your answer is YES, then one of two things is true:

A) You are lying to the other human being
B) You are lying to yourself.

Either way, you are a liar!

The swapping of body fluids is a very intimate experience. Think about it. You are taking INTO yourself fluids that have traveled through someone else's entire body and been imprinted with their biological and psychological signature, aka DNA. This "other" signature then merges with your own fluids to travel through your entire body, altering, even if for just one nanosecond, your signature. That is deep. No pun intended.

Short of rape, it takes a great deal of mutual chemical stimulation and physical proximity to induce the disrobing process that allows for coitus. Both pairs of eyes must be aroused through optical stimulation, which in turn sends positive charges to the brain's synapses alerting them to prepare for sexual warfare. The message gets adrenaline flowing as the heart gets over eager, pumping at who-knows-how-many bpm with anticipation.

Overwhelmed with euphoria, blood is expelled from the kardia traveling to the reproduction organs, tenderizing the nerve endings that will be on the frontlines. The nerve endings, pregnant with blood and bursting at the linings, beg for release; and nature takes over to provide repose. Disrobing quickly follows in an attempt to alleviate the sudden increase in body temperatures. The feminine legs involuntarily part to present the labia-guarded-cool-oasis that is the vagina, to the overheated, taut and throbbing penis. Coitus!

So how one can convince oneself as having successfully backslid from that coital experience into the black hole of "just friends" in under an hour is beyond me.

Shutting Her UP

1)   Feed her, but be careful. Not all foods will do. Some, like Mexican, are liable to result in more chatter.

2)   Stick a cup of hot Jasmine green tea in her hand and let the mechanical relationship between cup and mouth ensue.

3)   Throw a German man into the mix, sit back and watch what happens.

4)   Kiss her. Yes, kiss her. The seldom occurrence of this form of intimacy is guaranteed to leave her senseless for at least seven seconds.

5)   Pay her a compliment. It need not be genuine, but it will work.

6)   Tilt her head and get her to look into your eyes. This will disarm her and make her want to leave the room.

7)   Lie to her. If she doesn't trust you, she limits her vocabulary to "uhum."

8)   Be kind to her and she will sing for you. But avoid this option if you detest music.

9)   Toss in a CD with African beats and watch her recall her past life as the village seductress.

10)   Embrace her. She likes to listen to the beat of another's heart. Thankfully she knows that she must be silent to follow its rhythm.

11)   If all else fails, and ONLY if all other options are unsatisfactory, result to this option: storm into her bedroom

and head to the night stand. Reach underneath the bottom drawer. There you will find a button. Press it! This will unlock a small compartment on the far right bed post. Here you will find a small box. Open the box and take out the key. Go into the bathroom and use the key to open the far left bottom drawer. Inside you will find a green first aid kit. Open it. Inside you will find a thermometer, a needle and thread, 8 packs of orthro-tricycline, a ball of cotton wool, a pair of tweezers, some pennies (none of which are necessary for this option but I feel you need to know just to ensure that we are talking about the same box). There will also be a map in that box. Use it to find your way back to the bedroom and the night stand. It will direct you to the bottom drawer, yeah, the one you were in earlier. Here you will find a condom. Take it and go back into the living room. Sit across from her, staring dead into her eyes with the condom on your lap. One of two things should result from this:

a) She will lean in and kiss you, meaning all talk is done or
b) She will excuse herself, meaning all talk is done.

WARNING: This is an extremely volatile tactic that might backfire, resulting in either a verbal blowout or spending more time in each other's company, hence more talk.

Let's Talk About Sex

Why? Because your teen has discovered that she can do a lot more with those hips. She can shove them into crotch-smothering tight jeans and create havoc. WHAT!?

We all remember our teenage years when pimples and burning loins were commonplace. As if that wasn't hard enough (no pun intended), Hollywood, Bollywood and all other woods were over-sexing everything. Everything had a sex angle. The type of beer you bought determined how many women you'd bang that night. You name it, they attached a crotch to it. Hence the term "sex sells."

Throw yourself into a '80s or '90s movie flashback and all you get is the human "Basic Instinct." Sex came with a cheesy saxophone track, steamy windows, foggy ambiance, delicious sweat trembling down toned caramel skin and waterfalls symbolizing the moment of rapture. Everyone having sex seemed to be having fun, as was implied by the post-coital glow regardless of how fatal the attraction. They made it look like touching heaven. After one of those movies you couldn't wait to go out and get some.

Sex was everywhere. Even Pepe Le Pew couldn't get enough. And yet with sex in abundance you were not allowed to mention sex, let alone engage in it. Only loose girls and fast boys were allowed to touch heaven.

The kids are confused. Wouldn't you be? Adults who run these "entertainment" industries are creating these movies for teenagers while other adults purchase the equipment that allow the hot-blooded teenagers to view said content. Why then do they vilify them for shaving their heads and popping out babies with unknown backup dancers?

Can humanity afford to be any more sexually repressed than it already is? This morality stick is not only ridiculous but it has made us hate our nature. Africans, who spent the better part of the 20th century with tits and genitalia in the wind, are now covered up in batik-Kentecloth because cotton is the new flesh. Dare to mention returning to nudity and you will be doused in petrol and set ablaze.

Self-hate anyone?

Native Juices

There is something to be said about engaging in the consumption of native juices. Something about the exotic completely stimulates and titillates the senses. No, I do not speak of wild berries in the Amazon or nuts roasted in the Congo. I speak of something more sublime and sensual: human juices.

The inhalation of native body fluids through the various coital configurations is man at his most inquisitive. This endeavor over and under unchartered waters does more than just satisfy our carnal desires. It ensures the continual evolution of mankind by infusing the best of both races into a single organism.

Never marry someone if you have a moment of hesitation, might be suffering from a bout of malaria, or have never sampled native juices. Something about native juices gets a person fucked!

Accidental Pregnancy

The term *"accidental pregnancy"* is the stupidest pairing of two English words I have ever encountered. To label a pregnancy accidental is to openly state that one was/is unaware of the fact that the primary purpose of sex is procreation. Therefore, having an accidental procreation while engaging in sex is ludicrous. A fetus may be unintended or unwanted, but it is certainly not accidental for semen has always swum towards the ovum when fitted into a vagina. I'm just saying.

***

Look a wet t-shirt is just that.
A wet t-shirt!
It's not its fault it's wrapped over a pair of perky breasts.

***

The Methodology of Feelings

It has been my experience that anything
rushed into is rushed out of
If it is emotionally charged into,
it will be emotionally charged out of
These methodologies utilize NO reason
All that is done is done because it
FEELS good and when it stops FEELING good
it is no longer worth doing.

The Way of the Condom

She lifted up a pack of lubricated Trojan condoms and stated, "I am heading back to Kenya and these are coming with me. The question is are you coming with the condoms?"

He hesitated.

She turned her back to him and slowly bent over to pick up her suitcase. He now had a clear view of what else would be accompanying the condoms, his eyes glued to the place he enjoyed most.

She took her time straightening herself. Then she started for the door.

At that moment he could not deny that he loved the gentle swinging of her hips.

One thought ran through his mind, "Africa, here we cum."

Pre-Coital Agreement

And finally...at 3:43AM, we present a document that might help prevent all those unwanted pregnancies, baby mama dramas and the trapping of relatively sane people in loveless marriages for the sake of the baby.

DETOUR: The next person who calls a pregnancy "accidental" will get an earful from me.

Penis + Vagina = Semen dispersement (Ejaculation) x Ovum ambush (Fertilization) = Fetus

A thing doing what it is designed to do is no accident, merely brilliant engineering!

PRE-COITAL AGREEMENT

WHEREAS, _____ (hereinafter referred to as "Depositor") and _____ (hereinafter referred to as "Receiver") are currently pre-coital but wish to provide, prior to coitus, for a formal agreement ensuring that their separate lives will remain free from any claims arising out of the prospective coital relationship.

WHEREAS the Parties desire to contract with each other concerning matters of reproductive management during the term of their coital relationship and is intended to be a binding and enforceable pre-coital agreement and they understand and intend that the provisions of this Agreement shall prevail over the provisions of law or any jurisdiction that would apply in the absence of this Agreement.

1. CONDOM USE

A discussion regarding the use of protective gear must precede any disrobing.

I, the "Depositor", DO/DO NOT hereby consent to wear a silicone, lamb or plastic material over my member during coitus to provide an alternate receiver of my manly juices for the sole purpose of preventing the unwanted fertilization of "Receiver" ovum.

I, the "Receptor", do hereby consent to engaging in a coital relationship WITH/WITHOUT "Depositor" wearing a silicone, lamb or plastic material over Depositor's member during coitus to provide an alternate receiver of his manly juices for the sole purpose of preventing the unwanted fertilization of my ovum with the understanding that "Depositor" is released from any and all parental involvement and responsibility (e.g. financial, emotional, spiritual, physical etc) in the life of my offspring, in the event that my ovum is unwantedly fertilized.

2. MORNING AFTER PILL

Two Morning After Pills plus Instructions must be presented to Receiver pre-coital.

I, the "Depositor", DO hereby present "Receiver" with TWO MORNING AFTER PILLS (PLUS INSTRUCTIONS) to be consumed no more than 72 hours after completion of coital relationship for the sole purpose of preventing the unwanted fertilization of Receiver ovum.

I, the "Receiver", DO hereby confirm receipt of TWO MORNING AFTER PILLS (PLUS INSTRUCTIONS) which I choose to CONSUME/NOT CONSUME no more than 72 hours after the coital relationship for the sole purpose of preventing the unwanted fertilization of my ovum with the understanding that "Depositor" is released from any and all parental involvement and responsibility (e.g. financial, emotional, spiritual, physical etc) in the life of my offspring in the event that my ovum is unwantedly fertilized.

3. LOOP HOLE

In the event that "Receiver" does not reach orgasm, this Agreement is to be considered null and void and "Receiver" is free to go after "Depositor" for everything, you selfish son of a bitch!

4. NO INVOLVEMENT FOREVER

I, the "Depositor", do hereby consent to relinquish all parental involvement and responsibility (e.g. financial, emotional, spiritual, physical etc) in the life of the offspring in the event that "Receiver's" ovum is unwantedly fertilized, for the duration of my entire natural life plus fifty years.

5. AGREEMENT EXECUTED AS OWN FREE WILL

The parties agree that each enters into this Agreement without any reservations or promises, though there may be some pressure or inducements. They have done so on their own free and voluntary act and deed.

6. GUILT TRIPS & IDLE THREATS

If any disputes arise relative to the pre-coital agreement and the parties cannot resolve it, both parties agree that they will not result to guilt trips and idle threats.

7. AMENDMENT

This Agreement is binding and cannot be alterable by any custodians of the state, judicial or government entities without a mutual written Agreement signed by both Parties.

8. EXECUTION IN COUNTERPARTS

This Agreement may be executed in counterparts each of which when so executed and delivered shall be deemed to be an original and all of which together shall constitute but one and the same instrument.

9. BINDING ON SUCCESSORS

Each and every provision hereof shall inure to the benefit of and shall be binding upon the heirs, assigns, personal representatives, and all successors in the interest of the parties.

PARTIES SIGNATURES

_____

_____

Depositor _____   Date _____

Receiver _____   Date _____

*This Agreement is void if signed Post-Coital.
** Please make two copies.

What The Fuck!

An asshole is that part of the human body that ejects foul substances that would otherwise harm it. So, if someone calls you an asshole, take it as a compliment. Apparently you are providing a much needed life enhancing, service.

The Working Poor

I am 31 years old and I just woke up to the realization that I am part of the working poor. See that homeless man on the street? The one I just handed $1? The only difference between us is that I'm slaving for DWP, the gas company, Mercury insurance, Verizon, my job and my landlord (and here I thought feudalism was dead). Just like me, he too, may have 2 bachelor's degrees and no healthcare.

Here we are worrying about leaving no child behind; exactly where are we rushing him? HUH?! Is anybody telling them that a college degree is just that, a college degree? That fucking piece of paper ain't worth shit! You are better off dropping out right now and starting on your career of choice. I wish I would have asked for a GUARANTEE when they handed me my diploma on the f*&^%ing podium!

I'm sure I am not alone in my pissery. What are we going to do about this system that is manufacturing poverty at such an alarming rate? I want answers people. I want everyone who is running for office to tell me how we are going to stop our money from trickling UP. I want to know how many people fell beneath the poverty line and how many people became billionaires. How about that Fortune 500 and Forbes? How about adding those numbers onto your prestigious publications that celebrate men and women whose vanities feed off of the needs of the poor?

TV vs INTERNET: Which is more dangerous?

For those of you who believe the Internet, unlike the TV is less dangerous, corrupt and a better source of accurate information, think about this: Network and Media moguls, though cunning, are seldom stupid and rarely insane. But any mentally disturbed paranoid-schizophrenic with an Internet hook-up can log onto a computer and spray the web with their clozapine and Risperdal-laced rants, calling them facts.

Which do you think is a more dangerous source? The quiet voice stealing into the frontal lobe of a heavily medicated individual or the calculated thoughts of a man who knows that feeding the public what it thinks it wants, gets him what he knows he wants?

***

Some people live in a state of scripted reality.

Exchange of Opinions

Do you realize how self-centered it is to be so emotionally invested in fighting my ideas, as if my opinions have something to do with you personally? My opinion is mine and I will have it whether you like it or not just as you will have yours whether I like it or not. My point of view takes nothing away from you. Your opinion is yours and YOU get to keep it. I celebrate that.

I am not trying to change you. Please, keep your opinions.

This is merely a ***Dialogue*** -   an exchange of ideas.
                        Exchange -   barter, swap.

You can only exchange things ***that are different*** otherwise there would be no need for an exchange, now would there?

Please, breathe…it's not that deep.

Will You Marry Me?

"Nice and shiny, huh? It would look really good on your ring finger?"

"What? Ah yes, the cost. Well, a diamond like this is not easy to come by. I mean, mining expenses alone drive up the retail value. But for you, it will only cost…"

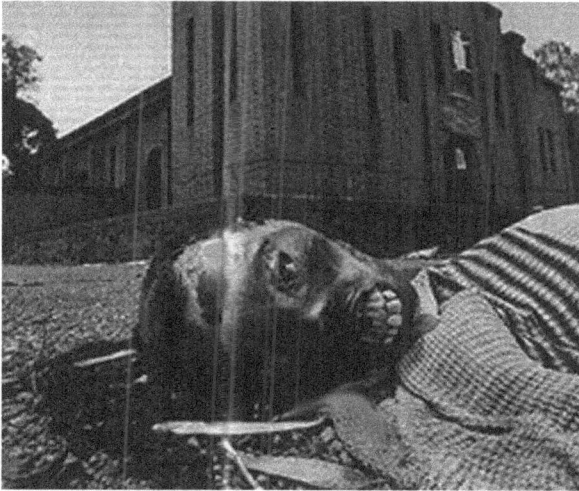

"Not so nice and shiny now, is it?"

"Oh, I'm sorry, I didn't mean to ruin your engagement."

Options

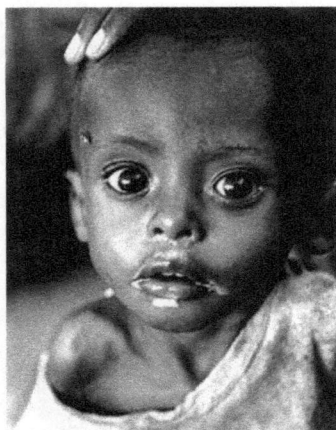

If at this specific moment, just as you are—financially, spiritually, mentally, physically, and emotionally—you had a choice between the two, which would you pick?

If you had the power to make anything you wanted in the world happen, which would you pick?

What Really Matters?

Traffic, tantrums
Cellulite, cell phones
Watch that Lexus
Exquisite wheel caps
Yellow bus rolling
Pregnant mother
smog smoking horizon

Broken homes and beat up wives
Do you like the odour from under my skirt?
Pelvic in the wind, kill the homos
Rape that b**ch, slap that a**
Nigger please! It ain't that big.
Colour, pigment, race, your life
Excuse my honky blue eyes.
Can the Chinese really see?

Sweat and tears
Sex no fears
Old generation hidden
New generation masturbates
Masticates and vomits
Booze and drugs
Food and fantasy
Leisure and duty

U turns
Y turns
3 point turns
Speeding on the interstate
Imitate life
Honk,
Break,
Screech,
IMPACT.
WHAT WAS THE QUESTION?

55

What The Fuck!

capitalism

What exactly is free about the Market?

Steel Plantations

You wake up every morning, wash yourself (hopefully), brush your teeth (probably), put on some clothes (definitely), and head out to a steel plantation where you slave for eight hours—minus the two fifteen minute and the one half hour lunch breaks you are legally allowed—to earn a small piece of paper with some numbers on it.

Upon receipt of this small piece of paper, you hop, skip and jump over to another steel plantation where you hand it over to a stranger who is equally enslaved, who takes it and puts it someplace safe with your number to identify it. You walk out believing it will be there when you need it.

You rush over to another steel plantation where you use a plastic card with more numbers on it to purchase food filled with high fructose corn syrup. This plastic card allows this plantation to take numbers from the small piece of paper that you were handed at your plantation, which you gave to a stranger at the other plantation to hold for you until you needed it. These numbers taken from your small piece of paper end up as other small pieces of paper handed to those people working in the plantations that grow the corn that makes the high fructose corn syrup.

This government approved high fructose corn syrup proceeds to burn a hole in your stomach causing extreme pain, forcing you to run off to another steel plantation where a doctor resides. The doctor asks if you have a separate plastic card with numbers that guarantee he'll get a small piece of paper with numbers that he too can hand a stranger in another steel plantation to hold for him until he needs it. But you don't have this card with the numbers that guarantee his small paper because the small piece of paper you were handed at your plantation does not have enough numbers to afford the separate card that has now become law.

Defeated, you return to your steel plantation and park yourself in front of a box you bought with 50% of the numbers on your small piece of paper, numbing your senses while you wait for death to ease your pain.

And you had to go to college just to earn the right to this bullshit!

Illegal Immigration

Why Illegal Immigration? I'll tell you why. Simple arithmetic.

If 20% of the world's population utilizes 80% of the world's resources, what percentage of resources is utilized by the remaining 80% of the world's population?

A. 20% of the world's resources.
B. 10%
C. 100%
D. Whatever they can get their hands on.

The correct answer would be **A.**

20%, which is all that's left of the world's resources, will NOT be equally divided among the 80%.

If that 80% run out of resources, and trust me they will, where can they turn to for more resources?

A. Nowhere.
B. They'd be dead by then.
C. To the 80% surplus currently in the hands of the 20%.
D. Who cares?

If you checked all the options above you would be right. Those without the means to head off to the 80% will have nowhere to turn and since no one cares, they will subsequently die.

Migration is not a new phenomenon people. If life started in Africa how the heck did all the corners of this planet get inhabited?

If you want to change immigration globally you must first ask yourself "am I ready to be uncomfortable?" Because that is what it will take. You will have to vote into office leaders who will increase your taxes, so that a ton of coffee from Colombia or tea from Kenya costs your country $250 instead of 25 cents. Much like the weapons, electrical equipment and other agents of death flooding the "developing" world from the "developed."

The 80% don't live off of democracy and its fallacy. They need resources. And for that to happen, both capitalism and democracy may have to take a back seat to fairness.

The Exportation of Capitalism and the fall of Western Society

Okay, come along with me. We'll be moving really fast so if you fall, rest and start over! There's no need to hurt yourself.

Even in the absence of democracy, capitalism can thrive as is evident in the Chinese dictatorship. But democracy leads to fewer than two market options: capitalism or partial socialism. Since the option of capitalism allows for the creation of far more wealth than that of a socialist society, it becomes the more suitable option for governments and individuals alike. Where governments are concerned, a democratic and capitalistic government perpetuates open markets and free trade with the world.

Unfortunately, capitalism unlike socialism does not create an equal playing field for its players. The economic greed of the democratic capitalist nations not only sows the seeds of their own demise, but ploughs and waters the grounds that facilitate its inevitable death. The open market puts the poorer countries, dealing mostly in agricultural goods and services (the necessity), at the mercy of more powerful nations, trading in mechanical and biological goods (the luxury). This is the fertile ground that creates a great imbalance in the world market and the dire straits within each sovereign nation, most of which democracy and capitalism have been forced upon by western invaders.

The internal imbalance within these struggling states leads to discontent amongst its citizens and a malediction that fuels all forms of immigration to the ideal democratic, capitalistic nations of the west. The man who has nothing seeks to sit at the table of the man who has everything. With the influx of immigrants unwilling to assimilate comes the segmentation of society and the collapse of democratic rule. But democracy does not collapse in one failed swoop. No, it is a slow leak.

The Immigrant's desire to belong and his need for

autonomy in the new land leads to the segmentation of society when the newcomers gravitate towards their own kind, a consequence of xenophobia and human nature. This segmentation weakens the whole, as people identify with their countries or continents of origin instead of the state where they pay taxes. Once the state becomes "parts" instead of "sum of the whole," the plague trickles down to the government level. Governmental agencies are forced to succumb to the needs of the minority groups by implementing socio-political laws and programs that are counter-productive in their attempt to unify the nation. Programs like Affirmative Action and Political Correctness further align minority groups by alienating the majority groups.

These programs create deep discontent among the majority, breaking them into smaller groups of malcontents identified by their ideology instead of nationality, as is the case with other groups. At this point, few if any of the people are truly citizens but merely guests choosing to identify themselves with places they are no longer residents of, or ideas that make no sense in the grand scheme of things. The fabric of the state and the government is weakened and the nation has no need to defend itself for there is none to defend. In the end, the state dies.

Capitalism

The SIX Estates

The Monarch –	THE MONEY HANDLER (Banks)
The Royal Court –	THE CORPORATIONS (Corporations are people too)
The Feudal Lords -	THE GOVERNMENT (Kinda obvious)
The Serfs -	The Working Class e.g. You and I
The Slaves -	Migrant Workers e.g. Your nanny or gardener
The Untouchables -	The Homeless e.g. What's his name?

Viva la revolucion! Viva la differance!

***

All Aboard!

Blow the trumpets of Armageddon
Arch Angel Gabriel,
We are all safely in the hand basket
Ready for the journey to hell.
I don't think we'll be back anytime soon,
So don't wait up.

FREE MARKET

Free:	*Unrestricted*
Unrestricted:	No *charge*
Charge:	*Price* asked for
Price:	Amount of money a thing is bought or sold for

Free: NO PRICE

Market:	Place for *sale*
Sale:	Exchange of commodity for a price

Market: A PRICE

In essence, the free market ideology is a price system promoted as having no price.

I guess this explains the severe seizures and subsequent ex-sanguination in the manufacturing sectors of developing countries after a large dose of free market is injected into the veins of their infantile economies, an act commonly referred to as murder.

The Natural Progression of National Greed

At the dawn of time, all empires that thought to conquer the world called it Empire Building.

In the BCE, the Romans under all the Cesars labored to conquer the world, calling it Civilization.

In the early AD, the Vatican under every Pope sent forth its faithful to conquer the world in the name of Christiandom.

Early 1700s saw the French under Bonaparte attempt to conquer the world in the name of Imperialism.

Late 1800s, the English under Victoria sought to conquer the world through Colonialization.

In the 1900s, the Germans under Hitler almost conquered the world, calling it Restoration.

Then comes the 2000s; the Americans rush to conquer the world under The New World Order.

Things that make you go "hmm!"

Capitalism and Christianity

Take a closer look at this. Something tells me these are strange bed fellows.

Capitalism: The acquisition of wealth to show status.

Christianity: It is easier for a camel to go through the eye of a needle than for a rich man to enter the kingdom of God.

Capitalism: Look out for number one.

Christianity: Greater love hath no man than this: that a man lay down his life for his friends.

Capitalism: Profit! Profit! Profit!

Christianity: Take only what you need.

Capitalism: Christians are the biggest market. Mega-fests, books, music, movies etc.

Christianity: Jesus chased out the profiteers from the temple.

How can the most Capitalistic country also be the most Christian? You can point a finger at the Vatican as well.

Wake up and smell the hamas!

Capitalism rests on the shoulders of the haves who stand on the shoulders of the wants. It needs an obvious economic delineation to survive, much like we need water for life. To then think that the Western powers are interested in exporting democracy is a bold face lie. They are trying to solidify capitalism's status quo under the guise of spreading democracy. China contradicts Western ideology by being a thriving nation that is not democratic, so an argument that states that capitalism only thrives in democracies is a lie.

***

Equality is a pie in the sky

Human -   People
To Race -   Compete

Human race - people compete
Human race - people competing against each other
Human race - people competing against each other for
                     world's resources
Human race - people competing against each other for the
                     world's resources with the hope of winning.

Unfortunately the memo wasn't circulated. See, in any race, there can only ever be ONE winner.

Equality is a pie in the sky for as long as we call ourselves the human race.

Slave Masters

Do you wonder why you are broke, busted and disgusted? Here's a simple answer. Who are your slave masters?

MY MASTERS	YOUR MASTERS
Car Payment	_____
Landlord	_____
Electric Company	_____
The Gas Company	_____
Car and Home Insurance	_____
Cell phone Provider	_____
Gas	_____
Luxuries	_____
Groceries	_____
Job	_____
Credit Card	_____
Federal Taxes	_____
State Taxes	_____
Social Security	_____
Medicaid	_____
Miscellaneous Expenses	_____

Slavery increases the master's profit margin by keeping production costs low. How do they do that? Simple, keep the slaves overworked and underpaid. Your pay will never be a reflection of your labor if you do not radically change the system.

Truth

There are benefits to resting in blissful ignorance 'coz now I am awake and pissed as hell!

Adult Teenager

As a teenager (which can extend to the age of 30), life is all about dealing with the undulation of hormones manifested as either a severe outbreak of acne or complete malcontent with society. Everything hinges on the immediate reaction, decision, premonition, intuition, preposition, imposition and any other *ion you can think of.

As an adult (which can begin as late as the age of 40) you learn to leave well enough alone. Acne is but a heat rush easily covered up by any 0.5% salicylic acid containing concealer. The world will still suck tomorrow so why worry about it today? And all the *ions are ignored in lieu of a quiet night, a good movie, and someone you love.

***

Loving

Men/Women are not the enemy. How you understand the experiences in your life is key. Learning how to love each man/woman individually prevents collective condemnation.

There is no greater joy than to give a gift to a stranger. I dare you to try it. Buy a stranger a cup of coffee, a card, anything. If the stranger asks why, ask him/her why not. For all deserve an act of love just because.

Liar, Liar, Pants on fire

Yes, I know it is a hard pill to swallow; in fact it's down right impossible, but it is true. Your children are liars! Long have we thought them "beautiful bundles of joy," and I use that term loosely. But we need to get off that cute syndrome and face the facts. Your kids are nothing more than short adults. Whatever you do, believe me they are capable of doing the same if not worse The only difference is they know that they can get away with it based on their looks.

∗⋈∗

Two Face

Doctor Jekyll in your face and Mister Hyde behind your back is a thing to behold. I quite wonder how the idea came to Bob Stevenson. I would not be surprised if the premise of his book was inspired by someone in his inner circle, if not himself. I, for one, believe that one does not need a potion, for all men exhibit split personalities without medicinal provocation. It is because of this that I bare such mistrust for the person who is so certain of himself and is willing to confidently predict his actions in any hypothetical situation. In my eyes he is either an idiot or a comic. The latter is at least good for a laugh.

Letting Go

It had become clear to me that I knew too many people and it was time to get rid of some of them. This wasn't personal, it was strictly business. See, friends require maintenance of the time and money consuming kind. They need to be wined and dined and cell-phoned; and those with benefits need sex. But once you reach the tender age of 30, there's just so much sex and texting you are willing to engage in. At the rate of 10 cents per text, the shit adds up. And don't get me started on the price of condoms.

But house keeping friends isn't as simple as taking out the trash. No. Very often there are feelings involved. Feelings that usually lead to some sort of optical leakage and pelvic lubrication that must be handled by the said friend getting their walking papers. In short, things tend to get a wee bit sticky! Like all things that stick, the best remedy is the one applied to a two-day-old band-aid. Rip the sucker off! It may sting a little, but the optical leakage is minimum and there's virtually no pelvic lubrication, at least not in the first 24 hours.

So it was that I embarked upon applying the band-aid theory to situations of my own making. But anyone who has ever had a scab can predict what happened next. Yes, the continual picking. Picking at it! There seemed to be a grand disconnect between my reasoning and feeling faculties. I thought the quick ripping and the minimal optical leakage was where it all ended. I even gave myself a grace period. Remember the 24 hours? Yes, I factored all that into my equation. 150 days later, I was still watering my cheeks! WTF? I guess someone was right when she said, "a theory is just that, a theory. Practice is something totally different." Oh, I guess no one said that.

Los Angeles IS the city of angels

I am tired of out-of-towners who come to LA for a visit and disrespect Angelenos.

First, fake people are EVERYWHERE in this world. At least here you can tell them apart by their boobs and lips, so count that as a blessing.

And second, if Angelenos having either their headshot, spec script or capezio dance shoes on the ready annoys you, stop and think for a moment about where you are. THIS IS HOLLYWOOD - ENTERTAINMENT CAPITAL OF THE WORLD! Artists have to hustle for every gig or go hungry. And the tools of our trade are--- please see above. If we were in Pittsburgh (50 years ago) everyone would have a plaid shirt and a hard hat. If we were in Miami (now), everyone would have an STD and a six-pack.

And finally, where can one find a gathering of people resilient enough to continue pursuing their dreams after multiple rejections? Los Angeles, California. This is the City of Angels not because some of the folks here are cute, but because Angelenos continue to dream and believe despite insurmountable odds.

On the verge of truth

I grew up in the black and the blue
that is all I know, the black and the blue

I am an immigrant

I have cradled another woman's loins in my mouth
Do you ever wonder what it is like?
The feeling of one who is like you lying with you?
I loved being loved but I hated the secrecy and the sin.
The feeling of shame, of being away from the truth, being
away from the Lord God, whom I worshipped every day.

It began with a sexual assault and 13 men later
I am emptier than when I begun.

I loved this man.
I would give him the world
I felt that he was mine then he left and that simply hurt.

What is love?
1 Corinthians 13:4-7
That is love.
Any questions?
You bet your ass.

Africa

Never before has one continent been so raped for the benefit of the rest of the World.

Weep my Africa for the sons and daughters you bore to build distant lands.

Weep my Africa for your tea, coffee, pyramids, wildlife, oceans and sands.

Weep my Africa for the diamonds tainted with the blood of your warring sons.

Weep my Africa for gold streams that have sent your children into caves never to return.

Weep my Africa for the uranium you gave to level the cities of Japan.

Weep my Africa for the puppets in power played by other's hands.

Weep my Africa for all you give and for the nothing they have earned.

Weep my Africa, maybe then, the world will understand.

Laundromat

There is something sad yet refreshing about this dance and I can't help but lend a hand, suggesting he separate the woolens from the delicates.

I am sitting in a laundromat watching the bachelors labor at their tasks. One throws back his ponytail and shoves blue towels into the washer. Another folds green sheets, another agonizes over the purple throw too large for the machine. With spectacles hanging off his nose, he starts to match his socks. He is bound to lose one, but I will not tell him that.

Across from the men, women labour over their dirty laundry. The divide is more than physical here. None speaks to the other, gazes locked in busy-ness. No one dares to steal a glance. These humans refuse to connect, as if looking into a mirror and seeing nothing.

The older man with the beautiful sea blue eyes leaves. He gives me I smile. I take it. Ponytail guy is agitated. Maybe he does not want to be here. Maybe, in the back of his mind, he thinks "she is better at this than I," if "she" even exists for him. Beanie man sits in the corner, watching. I wonder if he notices that I'm doing the same. Specs dude continues to fold.

Natalie Grant's song comes through my earpiece and I am distracted. I break into dance and all is forgotten. They watch. I do not care. I am alive and I know it.

9 to 6

Boredom is a dangerous tool. In the wrong mind it could cause irrevocable damage. For instance, at this very moment, I am wondering how to best induce self-asphyxiation without drawing unwanted attention for the sole purpose of "shaking-things-up." It is 4:00pm. I stand corrected, it is 3:00pm and I am desperate for purpose.

**THE END IS ONLY A PRELUDE
TO THE BEGINNING**

I would like to thank my Dad whose insistence that I grow up to be a lawyer taught me how to fight for my own dreams at a young age. Thanks Mom for giving me part of your personality, Michael for the quiet nights, Rita, Lynn, Dave, Yvonne, Donovan, Delvin, Krys OG, Chris W, Lynn O, Kulinda D, Princess, Tete and the men who inspired these rumblings. Thank you America for being my second home. And thank you Cetywa who sifted through a mountain of writings, book covers and fonts. Aherou gi chunya te. Alemo ni Were owoth kodwa nyaka chieng' moluongwa.

AUTHOR BIO

Peres Owino is a Kenyan born actress, writer, and dancer. She has starred in over two-dozen plays, playing three of theater's most coveted roles: "Hamlet," Lysistrata," and "Lady Macbeth." She is a multiple award winner and an LA ovation award nominee.

Her latest credits include a lead role in Simon Brand's feature film *Default*, a co-starring role in the FX TV show Terriers, and her own original play Cut at the Walt Disney Concert Hall, an official selection of the Redcat Fall 2010 Studio, which she directed.